PRESENTED BY

a Friend

A New True Book

EXPERIMENTS WITH ELECTRICITY

By Helen J. Challand

CHILDRENS PRESS ®

CHICAGO

Touching a static generator can
make your hair stand on end.

Library of Congress Cataloging-in-Publication Data

Challand, Helen J.
  Experiments with electricity.

  (A New true book)
  Includes index.
  Summary: A discussion of the properties of
electricity, with several related experiments, and an
introduction to different kinds of batteries.
    1. Electricity—Experiments—Juvenile literature.
[1. Electricity] I. Title.
QC527.2.C48 1986   537'.07'8   85-30887
ISBN 0-516-01276-2

TABLE OF CONTENTS

Everything in the world—living and non-living—is made up of atoms.

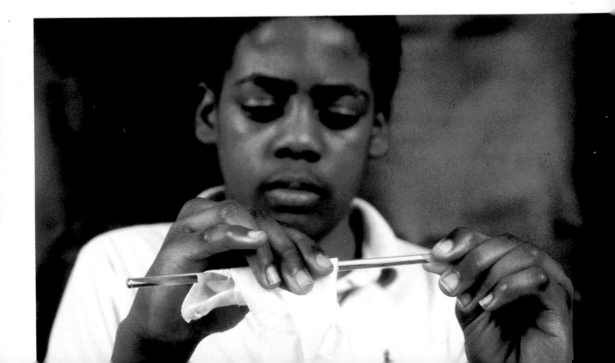

LOOKING ON THE INSIDE

It is easy to explain what electricity *does,* but very hard to explain what it *is.* To understand electricity you must understand the atom.

Atoms are the smallest parts in all material. A car, a tree, and you are made of atoms. They are so small one cannot see them. A microscope would have to make them millions of times larger for us to see. If everything in the whole world were broken up into kinds of atoms, how many different piles would there be? There would be 106. It is hard to believe so many things are made from so few kinds of atoms.

Student examines the chart that describes each atom.

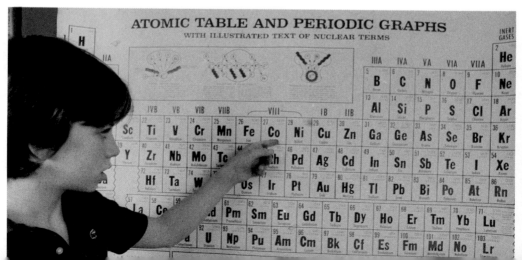

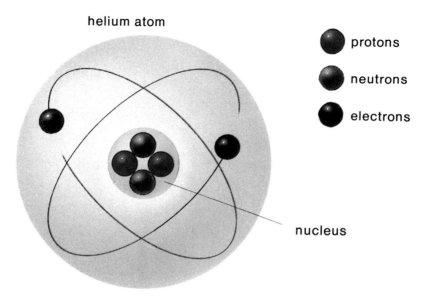

helium atom

protons

neutrons

electrons

nucleus

An atom is made of three kinds of tiny bits or particles. The center of the atom is a nucleus. It holds two types of particles, the protons and neutrons. Electrons, the third kind of particle, circle in the space outside the nucleus.

Usually an atom is neutral, for it has the same number of electrons and protons. Study the pictures of these two atoms. When an atom of sodium and an atom of chlorine come together they form table salt.

Table salt (right) is made up of atoms of sodium and chlorine.

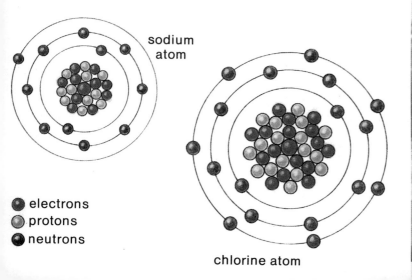

sodium
atom

electrons
protons
neutrons

chlorine atom

HERE COMES THE CHARGE

Electrons hold the secret to electricity. They have a negative charge. Protons have a positive charge. Neutrons have no charge and are neutral. The electrons in some are free to move. Remember they are flying around in the space outside the nucleus of an atom. Electrons can leave one atom and move

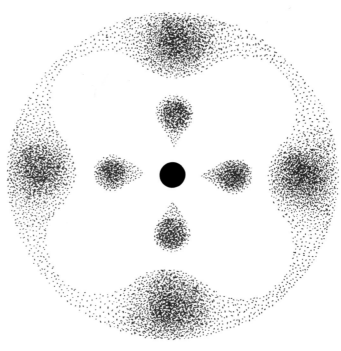

Drawing of an electron cloud. Electrons have a negative charge of electricity.

to another atom. This second atom loses electrons to the third one. All this movement causes a charge.

The material that picks up extra electrons is

negatively charged. The object that loses the electrons is positively charged. Atoms with the same charge repel or move away from each other. Materials that have different or unlike charges will attract or move closer to each other. An object that has a positive or a negative charge will attract a neutral material.

STATIC ELECTRICITY

Static means stationary or not moving. One form of electricity is made by rubbing two things together. This causes friction. The electrons will jump from one material to another and then stop. They will not keep flowing to form a current of electricity. Here are a number of ways to make static electricity using friction.

Young scientists experiment with static electricity.

Rub a comb with a piece of wool or fur. Some electrons will leave the wool and go to the comb. The comb now has more electrons. It is negatively charged. Bring it close to your hair. The comb is attracted to it and causes the hair to stand on end, if it is short. Soon the comb will become neutral and lose its charge.

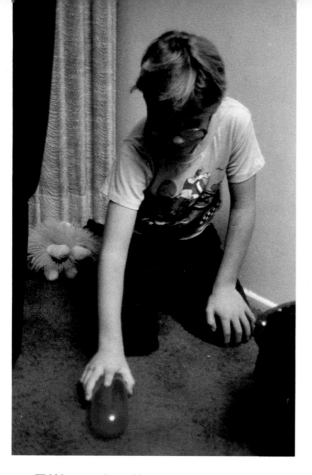

Fill a balloon with air and tie
it. Rub it several times on your
clothes or on the carpet. The
balloon will pick up extra
electrons. Touch the balloon to a
wall. Will it fall if you let go?
This shows that an object with a
negative charge will be attracted

to material with no charge. How long does the balloon stick to the wall?

Use a piece of nylon to rub a comb. The friction will cause the electrons to leave one object and go to the other. Which material is now carrying the positive charge? If you said the comb, you were right. It lost

electrons. Hold the charged comb close to a stream of water coming from a faucet. This shows that a positively charged material attracts a neutral material.

Have you ever gotten a shock inside the house on a cold, dry day? When you shuffle leather-soled shoes along a thick rug you pick up extra electrons. You are negatively charged. When you touch a metal object, a spark jumps. You are now discharged. Why don't sparks fly on a humid day? The wet air pulls the electrons away before they reach the metal.

Lightning strikes the John Hancock Building in Chicago, Illinois.

A HUGE SPARK

IN THE SKY

A flash of lightning is a
form of static electricity.
Masses of air rise and fall

during thunderstorms. They rub against rain clouds. This causes them to become electrically charged. Lightning will occur when two objects of different charges get close to each other. A spark will fly from a negatively charged cloud to a positively charged cloud. It will also go from a charged cloud to the ground or from the ground to a charged cloud.

Lightning over oil tanks

Lightning tends to strike
the highest object in its
path. This can be a tree or
building. Metal lightning
rods are put on top of
buildings. The electricity
hits them first. The charge
is conducted to the
ground. You may have

heard that lightning never strikes in the same place twice. This is not true. Bolts of lightning may strike the same buildings dozens of times a year.

ELECTRICITY ON THE MOVE

Current electricity is different from a static charge. The extra electrons keep moving from atom to atom. This form of energy can be used and controlled. Let's see how this happens.

A simple electric circuit can be made with a dry cell or simple battery, bell wire, and a light bulb in a

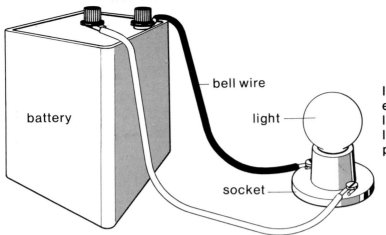

bell wire

battery

light

socket

In this simple electric circuit the light will stay on as long as there is power in the battery.

socket. Connect the dry cell to the light with the two wires. Be sure to take the coating or insulation off at the four ends of the wires. These are the contact points. When electrons are moving in a circle, the circuit is complete. The bulb will light up.

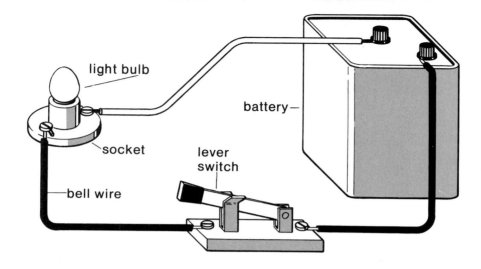

light bulb

battery—

socket

lever
switch

—bell wire

OFF AND ON

A switch is used to turn electricity off and on. It is connected in the same circle or circuit with the dry cell and light bulb. There are three types of switches. The first is a lever switch.

Use a piece of bell wire
and a knife or lever switch
to set up the circuit. When
the lever is up the circuit
is broken. The bulb will not
light up. Move the lever or
knife in the switch down
until it touches the metal
on the base.

Lever switch up—light off. Lever switch down—light on.

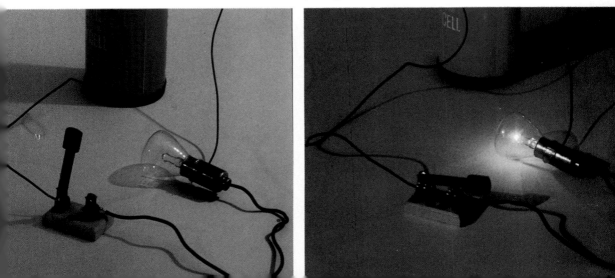

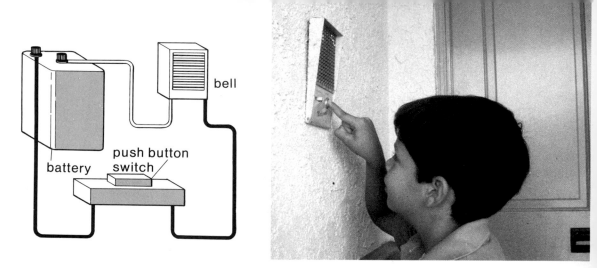

Pushing a button switch down closes the circuit and the bell rings.

A door bell has a push-button switch. When you push the button it closes a circuit. Only this time a bell rings instead of a light coming on. When you let go of the button a spring brings the button away from the base. This opens the circuit or breaks the connection. The door bell stops ringing.

A third kind of switch is called a snap switch. Move it one way and the lights go on. Snap it in the other direction and you are left in the dark.

Switch down—light off. Switch up—light on.

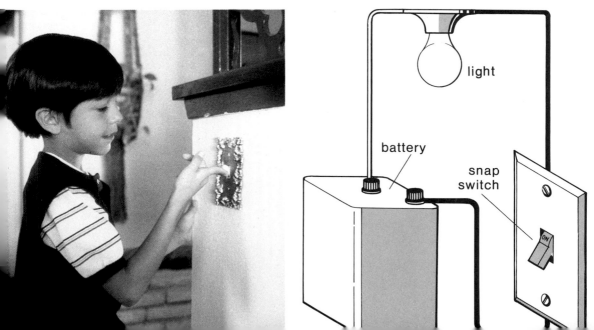

LIGHTS IN SERIES

A series means one thing after another. When lights are connected in one large circle, it is a continuous circuit. If one bulb goes out, the circuit is broken. All the other bulbs go out. Some Christmas tree lights are made this way. Here is how it looks.

The electricity flows through one bulb after

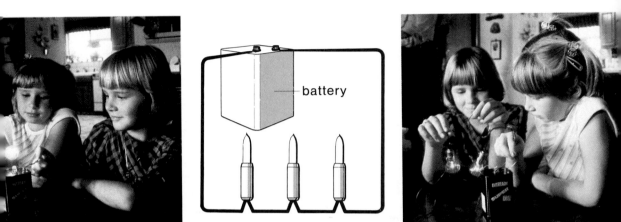

battery

Young scientists connect lights in a series.
With one bulb on a continuous circuit, the light is brighter
(far left) than it would be if two bulbs were on it.

another and then back to
the dry cell. There is only
a certain amount of
electric current. All bulbs
must share it. The more
bulbs that are put on a
string, the dimmer each
light becomes.

LIGHTS IN PARALLEL

Most lights and appliances are wired in parallel. Each one gets the full amount of electric current. If there were three bulbs connected in parallel, each would be as bright as a single light. One bulb could burn out and the rest would stay on. The circuits in homes, schools, and businesses are wired in parallel.

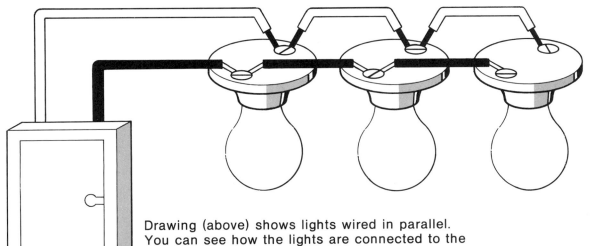

Drawing (above) shows lights wired in parallel. You can see how the lights are connected to the power source and to each other. Experienced electricians (below) are needed to install electrical systems.

31

CONDUCTORS AND INSULATORS

Most metals are good conductors. They will let electrons flow or move through them easily. Copper, iron, silver, lead, and aluminum are conductors. Carbon will conduct electricity, too. Acids, bases, and salts that dissolve in water, such as vinegar or a strong table salt solution, will also conduct a current.

Insulation covers the wires that conduct electricity

Material that is made of atoms that hold their electrons tightly are called nonconductors or insulators. They are used to stop electricity from going where it shouldn't go. Plastic, rubber, cork, glass, wood, cloth, and dry air are good insulators. Pure water is a

Electricians wear rubber gloves and use tools with rubber handles. This protects them from getting electric shocks.

poor conductor. However, many objects when wet make good conductors, even your body. Never touch an electrical appliance or light switch while taking a bath. If the insulation is poor you can be electrocuted.

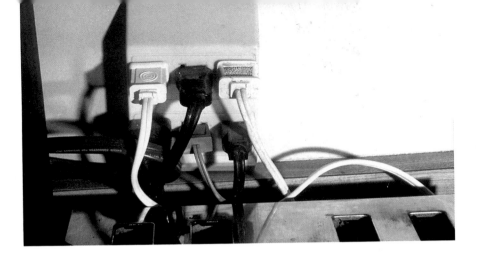

BLOWING A FUSE

Electricity going through a wire causes it to become hot. The more current, the hotter it gets. If too many lights and appliances, such as toasters and irons, are plugged into the same line a fire could start.

The fuse is part of the circuit in which electricity is flowing. When a fuse blows (above right), the circuit is broken.

A fuse is a safety device to prevent overloading. Inside the fuse is a strip of metal. It will melt sooner than other metals in the circuit, such as the wire. Before the line gets hot enough to start a fire, the metal in the fuse melts. The flow of electricity is cut off. Fire is prevented.

Circuit breaker (left),
unblown fuse (above)

Many places use circuit
breakers. They can be
used over and over. When
the line gets too hot, a
bimetal strip in the circuit
will bend like the lever
switch. This pulls away
and breaks the circuit.

HOW DRY IS A DRY CELL?

The 1½ volt battery used in science classes and the batteries in flashlights are dry cells.

A dry cell has three parts: a can of zinc, a wet paste of several materials, and a carbon rod down the center. One post or terminal is attached to the can. A second one is

When the materials or chemicals inside a dry cell dry up, the battery won't work.

attached to the rod. The zinc reacts with the wet paste picking up electrons from the carbon. Electricity is ready to flow. Wires can be hooked to the posts and the electrons move.

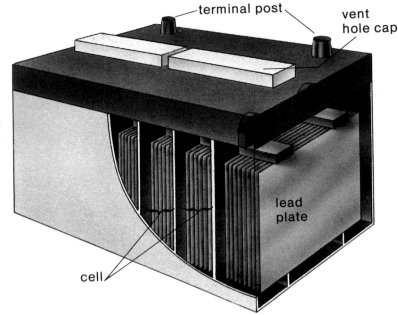

terminal post

vent hole cap

Most storage batteries have six cells. Each cell has two sets of lead plates. A sulfuric acid solution surrounds the plates.

lead plate

cell

STORAGE BATTERY

A storage battery is used in cars. It helps to get the car started and to run the radio. A storage battery produces electricity in the same way a dry cell does, only the chemicals are

Mechanic recharges a car battery.

different. It can store up energy. When it gets low it can be recharged. This can be done by running the car's engine for a while. It can also be recharged at a garage. A storage battery may last for years before it finally wears out.

SOLAR BATTERY

Do you have a toy or radio run by a solar cell? When light hits a solar battery an electric current is made. It has plates of an element called silicon. Solar cells don't wear out as do dry cells and storage batteries. The space program uses solar cells. Out in space the sun never stops shining.

The solar panel (top left) is used on the *Discovery* spacecraft.
This solar power plant (top right) provides electrical power in
California. Solar-powered watches (below left) and calculators
(below right) are common.

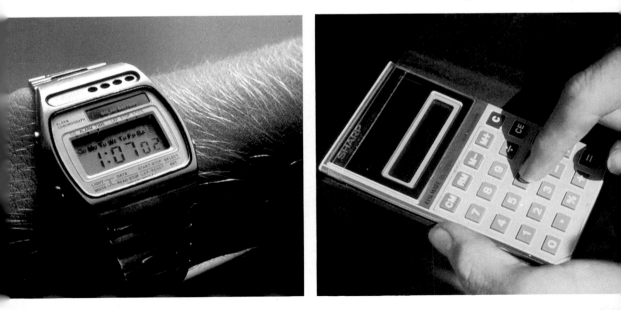

PLUG IT IN !

Have you ever counted the wall and floor plugs in your house and garage? Every room may have two to ten places to pick up a current of electricity. The kitchen, living room, bedrooms, bathrooms, and basement have electrical outlets.

What would the world be

A few of the many electrical appliances used in your home.

like if we couldn't plug
things in? Electricity is a
wonderful form of energy.
Some scientists say it is
the glue that holds the
world together. Wow! What
a thought that is.

WORDS YOU SHOULD KNOW

atom(AT • um) — the smallest part of anything that can exist alone

circuit breaker(SIR • kett BRAY • ker) — a safety device used to prevent overloaded electrical circuits, can be used over and over

conductors(kun • DUCK • terz) — materials that let electricity flow through them

electrons(ih • LEK • trons) — particles of matter, which have a negative charge and which circle outside the nucleus of an atom

friction(FRIK • shun) — the rubbing of one thing against another

fuse(FYOOZ) — safety device used to prevent electrical circuits from overloading; must be replaced after it cuts an overloaded circuit

insulators(IN • suh • late • erz) — see *nonconductors*

neutral(NOO • trull) — not charged electrically either positively or negatively

neutrons(NOO • tronz) — particles of atoms (along with protons), which have no charge and are neutral

nonconductors(non • kun • DUCK • terz) — materials that do not conduct electricity, used to keep it from moving where it shouldn't go

nucleus(NOO • klee • us) — the center of an atom, which holds two types of particles — protons and neutrons

parallel(PAIR • uh • lell) — an electrical circuit in which positive poles, etc., are connected to one conductor and negative ones to another, so the current flows in a parallel manner

protons(PRO • tahns) — particles of atoms (along with neutrons), which have a positive charge

series(SEAR • eez) — an electrical circuit in which current flows through all parts and then back to its source

static electricity(STAT • ik ih • lek • TRIS • it • ee) — electricity with stationary charges that do not keep flowing to form a circuit

INDEX

About the author

Helen J. Challand earned her M.A. and Ph.D. from Northwestern University. She currently is Chair of the Science Department at National College of Education and Coordinator of Undergraduate Studies for the college's West Suburban Campus.

An experienced classroom teacher and science consultant, Dr. Challand has worked on science projects for Scott Foresman and Company, Rand McNally Publishers, Harper-Row Publishers, Encyclopedia Britannica Films, Coronet Films, and Journal Films. She is the author of Earthquakes, Plants Without Seeds, Volcanoes, Experiments with Electricity, *and* Experiments with Magnets *in the True Book series and served as associate editor for the* Young People's Science Encyclopedia *published by Childrens Press.*